How to Succeed as a
NETWORK
MARKETEER

MARY AVERILL AND BUD CORKIN

KOGAN
PAGE

First published in the United States of America in 1994 entitled *Network Marketing*, by Crisp Publications Inc, 1200 Hamilton Court, Menlo Park, CA 94025, USA.

This edition first published in Great Britain in 1995 by Kogan Page Ltd, 120 Pentonville Road, London N1 9JN.

British Library Cataloguing in Publication Data

A CIP record for this book is available from the British Library.

ISBN 0–7494–1615–7

Printed and bound in Great Britain by
Biddles Ltd, Guildford and King's Lynn

Contents

Part 5: Prospecting

Preface

Network marketing is a business of the future. As with others, there are many pitfalls to be understood, but unlike many, there is tremendous financial potential if it is understood and operated correctly. Network marketing should be investigated by anyone who is interested in small business opportunities, a second source of income for their family, or the opportunity for financial independence.

How to Succeed as a Network Marketeer is a down-to-earth book written by people who have experienced the ups and downs of this industry and who have enjoyed extraordinary success in the business. The book is designed to cover three important areas of basic information with regard to the industry of network marketing:

1. What is network marketing and why is it such an exciting, talked-about, but often misunderstood industry today?

2. What should you look for and what should you be wary of in choosing an appropriate, successful network marketing company?

3. What are the day-to-day steps one needs to take in order to become successful in the network marketing business?

Good luck in your new venture!

PART 1
UNDERSTANDING
NETWORK MARKETING

Network Marketing:
a Person-to-Person Process

'In the '90s, we won't go to the store, the store will come to us.'

Faith Popcorn, author, from the *Popcorn Report*

Network marketing is a means of individuals selling direct to people in their own homes or work places. These distributors sell the products or services of a company to which they have been introduced by a sponsor. The distributors in turn, as well as using and selling the company's products, tell their friends, relations and contacts about what is on offer, and enthuse them to join in bringing the goods or services directly to the consumer, and be sponsored in their turn.

Distributors receive a discount on the goods they order (whether for personal use or to sell on), and also get a small percentage commission on orders received by the company through people they have sponsored into the network. The eventual user pays no more for the goods than if they were bought in a shop, since the discounts do not exceed the normal retail mark-up on consumer goods imposed by high street shops.

Word-of-mouth, people-to-people marketing is a powerful and cost effective approach to garnering market share.

Network marketing refers to direct selling through a network. *Multi-level marketing* is a multiple-level sales compensation plan. Sometimes the words are used interchangeably.

Direct selling, including matrix sales, multi-level marketing or network sales, refers to direct person-to-person sales. Right now, there are half a million people involved in direct selling, which, according to the Direct Selling Association (DSA), moves approximately £189 million-worth of products through the market annually in the United Kingdom alone. The DSA in America has approximately 150 corporations in its membership and recognises approximately 5.1 million salespeople. Sales through this method in the UK last year rose by 53.6 per cent over the previous two years. The number of people involved in direct selling has gone from 3.6 million in 1987 to over 5 million in 1992. It is enormously successful in other countries as well.

The Organisational Structure

A network marketing company normally has two essential parts: the *administrative organisation* and the *distributor organisation*.

The company (the administrative organisation) generally carries the following responsibilities:

- Market analysis
- Product research
- Product development
- Packaging
- Warehousing
- Shipping
- Distributor and customer service
- Distributor commission pay-out
- Development and management of national and international expansion
- Accounting/reporting
- Managerial reporting for administration and distributors
- Government relations

The administrative organisation generally has no responsibility for the direct selling of products − that's the job of the distributor organisation.

An independent distributor generally has three basic rights:

1. To buy products on wholesale terms
2. To sell products on retail terms
3. To sponsor new distributors into their organisation and, therefore, receive a commission on the sale of products by these other distributors.

The following diagram illustrates how an independent distributor organisation is structured:

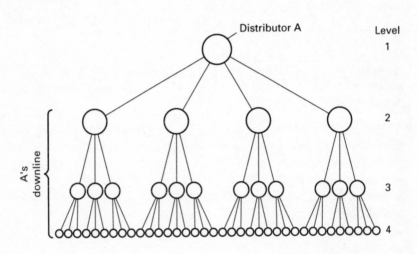

People introduce the business to others who, in turn, introduce the business to still more. Distributor A may never have met Distributor D; nevertheless, Distributor A may still be paid a percentage of Distributor D's wholesale purchases. This is known as the gearing of time. The organisational structure grows, and in time, exponential growth is possible. Normally, the administrative organisation tracks relationships and productivity by computer, and then gives computer reports to distributors on a monthly basis.

The distributor's job is to:

- Retail products
- Recruit and build a distribution organisation
- Teach, train, coach, and motivate.

Since the administrative organisation does not sell the products or services directly to the consumer, it is willing to pay generous commissions to independent distributors who build effective distribution channels. Network marketing companies pay distributors not only on the direct sales that the distributor makes, but also on the sales of other distributors in his or her downline organisation.

How to Succeed as a Network Marketeer

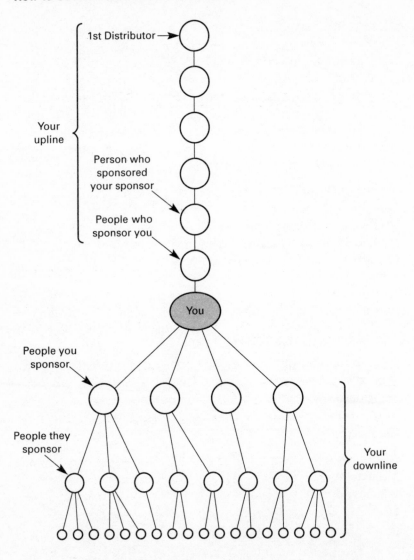

Your downline is all the people who came into your personal organisation, and all the people who are linked to someone that you sponsored. Your upline is all the people to whom you are linked, all the people whose organisations you are in. The economic reward relationship is with your upline and downline.

A Geared Income Vehicle

'I would rather have 1 per cent of a hundred people's efforts than 100 per cent of my own.'

J Paul Getty, billionaire and industrialist

Compensation plans and organisational structures may vary dramatically, but one characteristic that all network marketing companies have in common is gearing.

There are basically two kinds of gearing in business: (1) gearing of capital, and (2) gearing of time. In network marketing, gearing is receiving a percentage of other people's work, namely on your downline's wholesale purchases from the company.

Many people cannot get ahead because their job or small business consumes so much time. Time gearing is one way to get ahead. Give yourself a value per hour, then fill in the blanks to find your current income cap.

$$ £/\text{hour} \times \frac{24}{24 \text{ hours}} = \frac{£}{\text{Your Current Income Cap}} $$

When the total product sales in your organisation multiplied by your commission percentage is greater than you could produce alone, you start getting ahead, and you can use that to get ahead some more.

So many people are becoming interested in network marketing

because it removes the cap on income potential – with little or no capital risk.

Quiz

Yes	No		
——	——	1.	My ultimate goal is to be my own boss.
——	——	2.	I have set a specific yearly income goal.
——	——	3.	I have established a reasonable timetable for meeting my financial goal.
——	——	4.	In my answer to the equation above, I am dissatisfied with my current income cap.

(You should be able to answer yes to each question.)

Market Trends Point Towards Network Marketing

We are currently experiencing the convergence of a number of trends that have dramatically enhanced the attractiveness of network marketing.

Downsizing the UK manufacturing base

A job in UK Ltd no longer comes with a guarantee. In unprecedented numbers, those once solid organisations which had an unspoken contract with their employees for lifetime tenure, are now backing down. In the last few years in the UK, 3 million jobs have been lost and the replacement incomes are considerably lower.

There are thousands of highly skilled senior executives, middle managers, and sales and service-oriented individuals who are looking for jobs. These men and women are turning to small business alternatives for control over their lives. Network marketing has great appeal for them and they represent a ready pool of potential distributors.

Upturn in entrepreneurship

Since the advent of the interactive personal computer, the world has seen an unprecedented increase in enterprise. People look for small businesses because they represent the best economic return available in our society. Most people who venture into their own businesses are between 30 and 50 years old, which is the current age range of our 'baby boomer' population – one-third of the population. Women, disillusioned from attempts to break through the corporate glass ceiling, are leaving to start their own businesses in unprecedented numbers.

For those entrepreneurs looking to start a small business, network marketing offers many attractive characteristics, including low capital risk and the ease of operation.

Low capital requirements

Unlike traditional small business, network marketing *requires* (tick any that especially appeal to you):

- ☐ No expensive legal, financial or accounting services
- ☐ No maintenance or overhead
- ☐ No employees
- ☐ No higher education
- ☐ No business experience
- ☐ No large amount of start-up money.

A network marketing business can be operated on little or no capital. Starter kits from network marketing companies generally range from about £15 to a few hundred at most. Initial investment in stock can range from nil to a few hundred pounds. However, the company is not allowed to accept more than a total payment of £75 (including VAT) in a distributor's first seven days, to cover enrolment fee, samples, stock and sales aids.

The requirements for success in network marketing are:

- ● Desire
- ● Commitment
- ● Action-orientation
- ● Integrity

- Positive attitude
- Willingness to help others.

Advances in technology

Network marketing has not always been as smoothly operated as it is today. The industry has markedly improved its operations because of the tracking and communications capabilities of computer systems.

E-mail, cellular car phones and fax machines, which improve the speed and efficiency of communication, have enormously enhanced efficiency in managing larger network marketing organisations.

Conference call capabilities and satellite conferences can link distributors and prospects anywhere in the world. Flexible distribution systems are allowing customers to receive products quickly, thus minimising the need to maintain large stocks.

Globalisation of the economy

There are no territorial limits in most network marketing companies. The word-of-mouth process moves products through 'circles of influence'. Those 'circles' have no territorial barriers, and can be used to advantage in the network marketing business. People who live in rural or depressed areas of the country can now have access to the stability of broad-based markets through network marketing. People who live in one country can do business in several countries and have an international operation with no overheads.

Personal autonomy and freedom

Most jobs or businesses have us tied to a boss and other employees, a fact that erodes our sense of autonomy. Network marketing is constructed with independent distributors: people there to help you because it is in their economic interest to do so.

An ageing population

In 1990, only 4 per cent of the European population was over 65. Today it is about 12 per cent, by the year 2020 that figure will be approximately 25 per cent, and fewer will work until 65. People are turning to network marketing as a second or alternative source of income, or 'safety valve', for their families.

Distribution channel alternatives

As Paul Zane Pilzer, author of *Unlimited Wealth*, said in the March 1992 issue of the US *Success* magazine, 'Manufacturing costs have fallen so much in the past two decades that today distribution represents 85 per cent of the value of goods at retail. Therefore, the greatest opportunities in the 1990s are for those who reduce the cost of distribution.'

When the cost of distribution is lowered, more of the price per unit is available to be put into quality of materials and ingredients – and to profit. Consequently, if a network marketing company chooses to have superior quality products, the cost structure allows it to be a fierce competitor relative to other companies that choose traditional retail distribution methods.

Because advertisers face increasing challenges to reach consumers, major consumer-related corporations are increasing the budget allocated to direct promotion versus advertising. Person-to-person communication is a more effective way to reach consumers.

Beyond franchising

It is estimated that within the first few years of operation, approximately 70 per cent of business start-ups fail, whereas 90 per cent of franchises succeed. Franchising is a viable option because the small business survival statistics are relatively good.

Many people turn to franchising because the successful franchise programmes have proven products, packaging, delivery systems and a training system, all of which enhance the likelihood of success. An individual might pay a franchise fee of £2,500–£100,000 or more, and will pay an ongoing percentage of revenue, normally between 5 and 7 per cent. In addition, a franchise will have a time-limited contract and, generally, a territorial limit as well. In the 1940s, when franchising was developed in the USA by the motor parts industry, it was not even considered moral, let alone good business. Later, once the food chains caught on, the popular acceptance became enormous. UK turnover from franchised sales is estimated to double between 1993 and 1998.

Network marketing

Similar to franchising	*Superior to franchising*
• Significant marketing power • Proven products • Proven operations approach • Proven training systems • Name recognition • Increasing acceptance	• No franchise fees • Little or no capital risk • No territorial limits • No contract time limits • No overhead • No percentage of revenue paid to franchisor

As a consequence, hundreds of thousands of individuals are migrating to network marketing each year, because the sophistication is growing, the technology has made it all so much easier, and the risk reward profile is unprecedented.

PART 2

WHAT TO LOOK FOR AND WHAT TO AVOID

Choosing Among the Options

It is imperative to understand clearly the potential pitfalls of network marketing. You need to be clear about what to look for and what to avoid in several important business categories. Remember as you read that there are always exceptions to any rule and you must look at a network marketing company in its totality, not just with respect to one single factor.

Check these factors

Before choosing a network marketing company, you want to investigate the following:

- [ ] Legality of the company
- [ ] History of the company
- [ ] Financial strength of the company
- [ ] Structure of the company
- [ ] Strategic plan of the company
- [ ] Quality of management
- [ ] Quality of the products
- [ ] Size and direction of the market
- [ ] Timing
- [ ] Compensation plan
- [ ] Stock requirements
- [ ] Training and support
- [ ] How you fit.

Tick them off as you tackle each one.

Legality of the company

What to look for

Legitimate business. First and foremost, get involved with a *legitimate* network marketing company, not with an illegal pyramid scheme. Although on the surface they can look alike, the following chart gives basic distinctions between what is a legitimate company and what is a possible pyramid.

Illegal pyramid scheme	*Network marketing company*
• Paid directly just for recruiting investors	• Paid only on product sold
• Often no product at all or product without real use or demand	• Product with real consumer demand
• Upline always makes more than downline	• Downline can make more money than upline
• Substantial capital requested	• Little or no capital investment
• Pyramids have a limited life, usually less than two years	• Company has been in business for a substantial period

What to avoid

An illegal pyramid. A scheme where the products are not relevant; where money is made on the recruiting process rather than on the product. Any company that appears suspicious should be investigated as a possible pyramid.

Pyramid example 1: No real product
Years ago there was a famous pyramid scam in which the company was supposedly selling cosmetics. In reality, the company received money from each new recruit and gave money to the distributor for each new recruit. The company advised the distributors that it would store their products since they were not really necessary to generate commissions. Money was made by recruiting distributors who paid for the right to recruit others. It was discovered eventually that there was not even adequate product in the warehouse.

Pyramid example 2: Paid for recruiting
You are invited into a network marketing company where a widget costs £10 wholesale and sells for £15 retail. You are told that it costs £6,000 to become a distributor. Of that, your sponsor receives £3,000 and the company receives £3,000. You are then able to sell widgets directly, and you are also able to sponsor new distributors. If you sell a widget you make £5. If you bring in a new distributor, you make £3,000. Because it is more lucrative, you spend all your time bringing in new distributors – no product moves because the product is irrelevant. In that circumstance, the sponsoring distributor is being compensated directly from your up-front fee when you are brought in, not on the products that are sold in the organisation.

Avoid illegal pyramids. The Department of Trade and Industry has a leaflet that can give you greater understanding of the distinction. When in doubt be wary.

Get rich quick schemes. Avoid any company that promises you massive earnings in a short time.

History of the company

What to look for

Time in. If you have a low tolerance for risk, or even if you are just looking for a company that will be here in five years' time, then look for one that has already survived the blows of being in business for a while.

We are often inclined to look for a start-up, ground floor opportunity as a means of getting in on the big pay-off. In reality, network marketing is a difficult business to manage from the administrative side, and the majority of network marketing companies go out of business within a few years. Find a company that has managed adversity and high growth.

What to avoid

Ground floor, brand new and exciting. No matter how good a product is, no matter how big a market is, if a company does not know how to manage itself for survival and growth, it won't survive. You want an experienced management team; you want to *avoid* ground floor, brand new and exciting unless the management is reliable. Whether or not the company will survive should be your biggest concern after whether or not the company is legitimate – and in network marketing, the odds are dramatically against ground-floor successes.

Financial strength of the company

What to look for

Strong conservatively managed finances. Ideally, you should choose a company that brings significant financial resources to a fast-growing market, and one that creates barriers to entry against the competition.

Find out if the distributors in the company which you are investigating are consistently paid correctly and on time. Ideally, find a company that separates the commission that is due to distributors into a separate trust deposit account, so that it does not spend the distributors' money before it is due.

What to avoid

Cash flow problems. Because many network marketing

companies are privately owned, it may be difficult to obtain specific, formal financial information, but you can obtain a Dun & Bradstreet report on companies to check for history of prompt or late payment of creditors. It is imperative that network marketing companies guard their cash flow. Particularly in high growth times, companies may experience cash flow problems due to an increase in demand for stock. Make sure that the company you choose can manage growth.

Strategic plan of the company

What to look for

Clear plan, approach to growth. Ideally, the company and its distributors should be able to articulate how, where and when the company's growth will take place.

What to avoid

Confusion and no plan. If you get a muddled response to the question, 'Where is the company going?', you need to look again. Without new ideas, new products, and strategies, the distributor population can lose enthusiasm; and that spells trouble for the company. If a company fails to plan, ultimately it is planning to fail.

Quality of management

What to look for

Ability and integrity. Because there is often a dramatic high-growth and high-income spurt in network marketing, some managers get involved in network marketing simply to take the money and run. Some owner/managers seek to build the business to the point where it hits dynamic growth, with the intent to shut the company down and pocket the cash rather than to reinvest in the company's or distributor's future.

Your turn: Do some research

Choose a network marketing company you are considering as a business opportunity. Before joining, you need to do research and carefully scrutinise the people at the top by asking the following sorts of question:

- What kind of people are they?_____

  _____

- What is their reputation for personal integrity? _____

  _____

- Are they in this for the long term?_____

  _____

- What is their commitment to taking a place in an industry, and to position their company over many years?_____

  _____

- What are their credentials, background, track records, experience, values, expectations, goals, philosophy?_____

  _____

- What is their involvement with distributors, availability to all levels, and demonstration of social and environmental responsibilities?_____

  _____

- Are they concerned about their distributor population?____

  _____

- What do distributors say about them?_____

  _____

- How do distributors privately view them? _____

  _____

- Do the distributors trust the management? _____

Find out if management demonstrates high standards, the ability to operate effectively, the growth of a dynamic business, and the commitment to a lasting position in the product market-place.

What to avoid

Poor managers and bad character. Your first impressions and intuition should not be ignored. Investigate carefully if an owner/manager appears to have a questionable appearance, integrity or character.

If a prospective company is headed by an entrepreneur who invented the product, look closely, because people with technical skills are often ill-equipped to be good business builders, but this is not always the case.

If the company is headed by someone who is involved in both the administrative and distributor organisations, conflicts of interest exist that will make it hard to manage the organisation.

Quality of the products

What to look for

Superiority and high demand. How do the products compete in their market-place? If they are 'me too' products, it will be a struggle to market them. If the products are clearly superior, the distributors will have a much easier time attracting new customers and new distributors. If products are just comparable in quality with others available in the market-place but have significant price reductions, then you must consider whether, and how long, the company can survive with smaller margins. Also, determine whether consumers really want the products. Without real consumer demand, the pipeline will fill up and backfire on you.

A necessary step is personally to test the quality of the company's products by buying and using them, and reading the labels and literature. Have the products gained industry recognition? What is the reputation of the products? Do you like them? Would you use them if you were not in the business?

You want to find a company that has a commitment to ongoing product research and development, and to regular product updates based on new available research. Thus, you are looking for a company that has a clear and strong reinvestment pattern for product development.

What to avoid

Mediocrity, pricing issues and single product companies. The last thing that a distributor wants is a *Which?* report placing his product third in a category. In addition, unless more, good marketable products are coming soon, avoid single product companies. With single product companies, you run the risk of new competition surpassing your product, and of customers getting bored with it. The balance of a multiple product line can greatly enhance sales and continuity of customers as well as stability in the business.

Size and direction of the market

What to look for

Large, growing, preferably with emotional appeal, greater diversity and preferably consumable. To avoid fighting powerful market trends, identify a strong, futuristic trend, such as health, fitness, wellness, anti-ageing, personal appearance, car products and soaps among others. Link these trends to a network company offering superior products in a growing market. Go with the trends, not against them. Seek a broad-based, mainstream, preferably daily use market, because your distributor population will be mainstream. Never under-estimate the psychological and market power of broad-based trends.

What to avoid

Stable or niche markets. Even large markets are not good if they have peaked, because they will not excite or drive distributors or customers. Be careful of those interesting, but small, niche markets. They just are not big enough to sustain a large body of distributors over time. Be concerned about durable goods, where the consumer buys once and seldom or never buys again in a market.

Timing

What to look for

The beginnings of dynamic expansion. It is said that 'timing is everything'. While it may not be everything, it is a major critical factor. Identify what stage of business the company is in. Affiliate with a company which is in or about to begin a high-return stage — that time in a company's life in which the growth is going to be extraordinary. For distributors who capture that moment, the return will be extraordinary.

What to avoid

Too early. If a company is new, it may be exciting because of its newness and potential for high growth. But you need to allow the company to prove that people will buy the products again, and that the company can manage the cash flow as it grows. Start-ups have numerous inherent risks: product risks, management risks, financing risks, etc. If it is truly a significant opportunity, the company will be around long enough for you to capture much of the upside sales, while avoiding the downside risk of a failed company.

Too late. If a company has not experienced growth for some time, and has not changed strategies in order to grow, it may be difficult to build an organisation because there simply is not enough excitement inherent in the situation. If a company has been around for a long time without periods of fast growth, there may be underlying reasons why growth will not take place.

Compensation plan (or marketing plan)

What to look for

Potential for extraordinary return. Compensation plans can look complicated and confusing at first. A compensation plan must have the capacity to pay a worthwhile income for your productivity. With some plans, the income potential is minimal. A simple way to determine economic potential is to review how well the leaders who have been in the business for a period of one to five years are doing. For example, have they been able to go into business full-time? A 'Yes' is an indicator that the plan probably has holding power to keep attracting players long-term.

Also, make sure that the compensation plan pays 'deep enough' in terms of levels of marketing groups. When you train and coach people, you should be compensated once they are successful, instead of having them 'roll out' below your pay-out levels. Find out whether the people at the top of the business make extraordinary incomes. This is a key motivator to the sustaining of your downline distributors and attracting new ones. The larger the potential for extraordinary return, the higher the likelihood of attracting into your business skilled and effective people who have been successful in other areas.

What to avoid

No long-term leaders, and too much pay-out. There is probably a flaw in the compensation plan if there are *no* extremely successful people within an organisation. If a company has no leaders who have been around for three to five years, it is because either the money rolls out below them, or they can't make money in the first place.

Avoid any company where the distributor begins a discussion about the business by telling you about the compensation plan. The promise of wealth should be in the context of a stable, growing company that produces marketable products. A marketing plan can be ill-thought out and created in a matter of hours. By itself, or as the lead item, a marketing plan does not make a good, stable business. For example, 'Our company pays out seven breakaway levels at 8 per cent and a total of 65 per cent of the wholesale pound.' Ask yourself: 'Can the company operate on the 35 per cent, or will they be out of business before I receive my 65 per cent?'

Percentages are less important than the long-term stability of the company. If a company speaks about its marketing plan first, there may be little else of substance behind it. Such a company may operate similar to a pyramid, moving quick money instead of growing a steady, stable business.

Stock requirements

What to look for

No requirement. Distributors should have the right to choose the level of stock that they wish to carry. Preferably, the company has a system that does not require the distributor to invest any or much capital in stock. Often the product can be delivered directly to the consumer or to the distributor within a period of days.

What to avoid

Front-end loading. Companies whose marketing plans are 'front-end loaded' need careful scrutiny. For example, if a higher title can be bought, or if products can be purchased *for* *less* by acquiring a significant amount of stock – like £5000 or more up front – you need to be careful. Problems can arise if a person buys a lot of product, puts it into storage, and does not sell to a consumer. A few months later, when the commission cheques have been paid on these products, the person may want to send them back to the company for a refund. This can create a crisis for the company cash flow and it can create an unhappy new distributor. Having a lot of stock in the pipeline but not sold through to a consumer can eventually undermine the financial viability of a network marketing company.

Training and support

What to look for

Lots of resources. You are looking for a situation in which the basics of the business can be learned readily. Ongoing, effective meetings and training are essential to the individual distributor's and downline's success. Ideally, the company and distributor network have communication tools for continual communication and involvement.

Uplines should be actively committed to their downline's success and capable of helping you. Quality tapes and manuals are enormously helpful. Investigate the tools and people available to learn the business. Who will your upline be? Are they successful? Will they help you?

What to avoid

No commitment to training or support. Training gives a structure for downline success. You are like the MD of your own network marketing activity; you are the leader of your own downline organisation, and you will only be as successful as your downline. Duplication is the process by which your business will grow. A simple business duplicated well among many people brings success. Avoid organisations that play down training, or that do only satellite meetings and never have live meetings. They will not succeed as well, or as fast.

How you fit

What to look for

Your own commitment. You are a critical piece of this network marketing puzzle. Find a company and a product line that you can be proud of and that you can see yourself staying committed to over time. Without your long-term commitment and consistent actions towards building the business, no one – no company and no upline – can make you successful.

Success will *not* be determined by whether or not an individual has a sales personality, a specific education, a business background, or an outgoing personality. The essentials are instead: a positive attitude, persistence and a willingness to learn and to work. This is a people business. Successful distributors enjoy people and enjoy helping others to succeed.

What to avoid

Misfit. If you just do not feel good with the people in the company, or if you cannot see yourself using or selling the products, the company you are investigating may not be the right match for you. Look closely before saying 'no', because products often grow on people.

Give yourself some time; often someone new to network marketing begins the business with a status concern: 'Is this beneath me?' He or she later develops prosperity and the love of helping others and becomes a staunch network marketing advocate. We often tell people that we had status issues too until we started to make more money than most managing directors.

What to look for and what to avoid
Do the following quick check to see how well you remember the 'look fors' and 'avoids' of network marketing. Compare your answers with the authors'.

	Look for	Avoid
1. A company with leaders who want to teach you the business and has training materials from which to teach.	_____	_____
2. A company with a single product.	_____	_____
3. A company that wants you to buy in to a higher level, a 'front-end load'.	_____	_____
4. A brand new, start-up company.	_____	_____
5. A company that will pay you directly for recruiting people who have not yet bought or used any product.	_____	_____
6. A company that pays only on products sold.	_____	_____
7. A network marketing company with a good, non-consumable product in a niche market.	_____	_____
8. A company that can spell out its growth strategy to you clearly.	_____	_____
9. A company with proven leaders and managers who have long-term commitments to distributors.	_____	_____
10. A company and a product line that you can be proud to represent.	_____	_____

Answers: 1. Look for **2.** Avoid **3.** Avoid **4.** Avoid **5.** Avoid **6.** Look for **7.** Avoid **8.** Look for **9.** Look for **10.** Look for.

PART 3
FIVE STEPS TO NETWORK MARKETING SUCCESS

The Five-Step Process

'If you don't know where you are going, you won't know when you have arrived.' This old adage holds as true for business as it does for day-to-day living. By following this five-step process, you will have all the tools and gain the confidence you need to become a network marketing success.

Step 1.   Create your attitude

Step 2.   Write your values, dreams and goals

Step 3.   Gain the basic knowledge

Step 4.   Understand business finances

Step 5.   Build your prospect list

Step 1: Create Your Attitude

Develop a positive attitude

A persistently positive attitude is critical to success in the network marketing business.

Because you attract people to yourself first, then to the products or the business, a positive attitude is essential. Without a positive attitude, you are less appealing to have around, and you cannot be the attractor that you need to be.

As in all small businesses, effort must be spent before rewards are achieved. To sustain yourself, a consistently positive attitude may make the critical difference between falling out of the business too soon, and making it all the way to financial independence. You must like and believe in yourself. If you don't, why should others?

List your winners
List five positive factors that you count on to keep an upbeat attitude:

1. _____

2. _____

3. _____

4. _____

5. _____

Beware of dreamstealers

'Dreamstealers' abound as you start your network marketing business. There will be well-intentioned friends or family members who believe and feel the need to tell you that 'It can't be done' or 'You're crazy'. You need to protect your positive attitude. Once you hold steady, those dreamstealers could choose to become a part of your downline. Your belief and your attitude can make all the difference, so it is important to check on yourself regularly.

Handling your dreamstealers

Complete the following exercise:

My possible dreamstealers   *How I'll handle them*

Name_____   Option_____

Name_____   Option_____

Name_____   Option_____

Name_____   Option_____

Name_____   Option_____

Options for handling dreamstealers

Option 1.   Invite them to look for themselves.

Option 2.   Ask them to pay my bills if I don't follow this income producing option.

Option 3.   Think of them as an educational challenge that will take time.

Option 4.   Know that they are who they are, love them anyway, and go on.

Option 5.   Cave in ... give up my dream because they said so.

Apply basic principles in your life

A positive attitude is a learned skill; it should be continuously developed by looking at each situation as an opportunity and viewed in a positive light.

A positive attitude creates a positive life. Once the basics of your products and your business are understood, your success or failure rests in large part on the management of your self-esteem. People buy from you because they like you. This applies equally to the marketing of cars or insurance and the network marketing of a business. A very interesting fact is that people will not like you more than you like yourself.

Therefore, to be successful you must like yourself. This can be accomplished by taking stock of your assets and affirming over and over again, 'I like myself', in writing and verbalising. Sound silly? Maybe so, but it works.

My daily affirmations

Do not underestimate the power of positive thinking. In the space provided below, list three affirmations to boost your self-esteem and attitude.

1. _____

_____

2. _____

_____

3. _____

_____

Transfer these affirmations to 3 × 5 index cards and keep them with you. Look at them often and read them aloud to yourself.

Step 2: Write Your Values, Dreams and Goals

Decide what is important to you

Before you start any new endeavour, it is useful to articulate for yourself what you value most in your life, to remind yourself about what's missing, and what you want to accomplish.

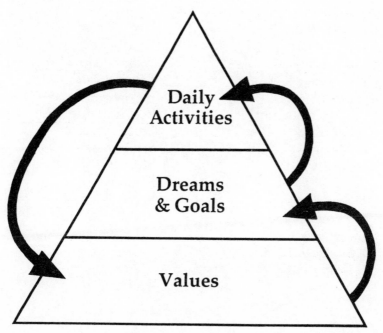

This is not always an easy process but it is always a useful one. Often we become frustrated because our day-to-day reality is not in alignment with our underlying basic values. If our day-to-day actions are in harmony with our values, we have a much greater potential for happiness.

Re-establish your values

Often people try to live their lives by doing a lot of tasks, without ever having a long-term direction. This is absolutely unsatisfying. Our values are our cornerstones. When starting a new endeavour, it is wise to review our values because they are the underlying framework for our lives. Once we have articulated what is important to us, we can decide, at the more detailed level, what our goals and tasks should be.

Key values

Tick the 10 values most important to you.

☐ Competence	☐ Organisation
☐ Contribution	☐ Perseverance
☐ Excellence	☐ Personal Growth
☐ Fairness	☐ Physical Health
☐ Family	☐ Playfulness
☐ Financial Security	☐ Positive Attitude
☐ Frugality	☐ Productiveness
☐ Giving	☐ Selflessness
☐ Hard Work	☐ Self-Sufficiency
☐ Honesty	☐ Sincerity
☐ Humility	☐ Spiritual Growth
☐ Innovation	☐ Stability
☐ Integrity	☐ Thoughtfulness
☐ Intellectual Growth	☐ Tolerance
☐ Leadership	☐ Tranquillity
☐ Neatness	☐ Truthfulness

Identify your values
Write your three highest values:

1. _____

2. _____

3. _____

Define your dream

They say that in network marketing, 98 per cent of the business is *why* you are doing it. Our dreams are our Whys. Why do you want this business? Why will you sacrifice to become successful? Articulate your dream for yourself – it will go a long way in helping you to become successful.

What is your dream?_____

_____

_____

_____

_____

_____

Now write the sentence or phrase that excites you to action, and that will go into your daily planner each day and every day to help you be more effective.

_____

_____

_____

_____

_____

_____

Write your goals

No significant achievement happens without goals. Deciding what we want may be a lifelong process, but goal-setting can speed up the process. Often the difference between setting and not setting goals is the difference between working smart and just working hard.

To succeed, think in terms of results. Before you set your goals, identify your strengths, weaknesses, your needs, and understand your values.

Successful people make two decisions in their lives. The first is related to goals. They decide on a goal and a time they will achieve it. The second decision that they make is what price they are willing to pay for achieving their goals. Remember, the price always precedes success. The bigger the price you are willing to pay, the bigger the success you will enjoy!

Goals

It is not enough to state vague goals; for example, 'Make more money', 'Get ahead in life', 'Get a qualification' or 'Expand my business'. Take it one more step: be specific.

Be specific.   **1.** *6 months* **2.** *1 year* **3.** *3–5 years*

Professional
1. _____

2. _____

3. _____

Personal
1. _____

2. _____

3. _____

Financial (salary, earnings, investments, possessions)
1. _____

2. _____

3. _____

Residential (buy, sell, expand, improve)
1. _____

2. _____

3. _____

Spiritual/Attitude
1. _____

2. _____

3. _____

Educational
1. _____

2. _____

3. _____

Physical
1. _____

2. _____

3. _____

Step 3: Gain the Basic Knowledge

As you start your new network marketing business, you need to become knowledgeable about the products, the company, the compensation plan and the industry.

Know your products

The single best way to learn about your products is to *use* them. If you are serious about the business, buy all the products if your company has a moderate product line, or buy the key products if you have a broad-based product line. Then migrate through the entire product line as soon as possible. This is necessary in order to tell people what each product smells, looks, feels and tastes like. That way you can share the benefits of the products *from your own experience*. Your belief level will go up once you are knowledgeable about the products.

Use the company's products *exclusively* whenever possible so that a visitor to your home does not see a competitor's products and lose confidence in your belief level.

Listen to and read all available material on your products. Ask your upline lots of questions about the products until you feel knowledgeable and comfortable.

Know your company

Read the company brochures and listen to any company tapes and videos. Talk to distributors. Visit the company if possible. Find out about those who own and operate the company, what their background is, what their philosophies are in the business, and how they view the distributor segment of the business. A business reflects the character and intentions of the people at the top, so ask questions.

Know your compensation plan

How is the plan guiding you to make money? What is the plan telling you to do to make money? Do not assume that you know how to make money in this business — listen to where the plan tells you to concentrate your efforts. Then do it. Also, find out where people get stuck in the plan. Most people do not really understand their own plan. Ask questions of your upline until you understand it and can therefore explain it to others, *simply*. Ask your *successful* upline what the plan is telling you to do and *not* to do. Simplicity is a good test of understanding in every aspect of the business.

Know the industry

Ask questions of others who have been in network marketing in order to understand the trends and to understand who the network marketing competitors are, what their strengths and weaknesses are, and how to handle them.

One of the most useful sources of knowledge is your own upline. Call them all, tell them you are very interested and excited about the business and ask if they could give you some hints. Then take their advice, tell them you took it, and return for more. If you return for more but do not take the first advice, your upline may be less open to you in the future.

Of course, the greatest teacher is experience. Take action, then assess what works and what doesn't. Tape yourself on the phone, video yourself if you give a group presentation, and ask for feedback whenever possible. Do two-to-one meetings with your upline and watch and listen to how they do the business. Go to training sessions and meetings whenever there is a senior person in your area. Although network marketing is a simple business, the complexity comes in the relationships with people; you should not expect to be as skilled at the beginning as you will be after the experiences of both success and failure have guided you.

Step 4: Understand Business Finances

Understand accounting processes

Forming a company to start a network marketing business is not usually necessary. A sole proprietorship or a partnership is an appropriate business structure unless you have special tax or organisational circumstances. With regard to product liability protection afforded by the corporate veil, most network marketing companies have an umbrella insurance policy for their distributors that protects them from product liability legal actions.

Starting your network marketing business as a limited company creates extra expense, time and reporting requirements that dampen the attractiveness and ease of entry. And since this is a business of duplication, the next person will do what you did. Thus, you want to keep it simple wherever possible.

An important benefit of network marketing is that for little or no capital you can create a small business which allows you to begin to take advantage of certain appropriate tax allowances.

As you start your business, it is a good idea to have a discussion with an accountant about tax allowances applicable to your style of running the business, as well as about the latest Inland Revenue rules. You might be able to claim allowances for a portion of your home, computer, car, travel, etc.

A bookkeeper or accountant can assist in setting up a simple accounting system. Bookkeepers are generally less expensive. Maintain a separate bank account and separate credit card for your business to avoid mingling business and personal expenditure, which would make for an accounting nightmare.

Eventually, adding a simple software accounting system to your computer may be useful. But do these kinds of thing *after* you are in action and have decided that you like and will stick with the business.

Be realistic about money matters

To avoid wasting money, determine to buy *only* what is necessary for the business. The multitude of available support materials can eat up cash and not advance your business one step. Listen to your upline about what it is *important* to buy, and about what can wait.

For people who are new to small business, it is important to understand the reality of the difference in cash flow between a job and a self-funded small business. In a job, a certain, regular amount of money comes in every week, or two weeks or month, no matter what people do or do not do, until or unless they get promoted, sacked or leave. Then, at the end of the year, there is, perhaps, a minor increase in that amount, based on merit or cost of living.

In your own start-up, you put in what seems like endless hours of effort and time to get the business off the ground with little return for the time invested in the early stages. The distinction here is that you are not paid for effort, you are paid for productivity. And there is much to be done in laying the groundwork before a business becomes productive in the sense of moving enough product through the market to make significant money.

> ## You have to start somewhere
>
> One distributor tells that when he started his business, to his wife's dismay, he worked hours and hours in his first month, and was very proud to call her when his first cheque came in. 'Honey, we made 875 this month.' Then he paused and said, 'The only problem is that the decimal is after the 8.' His wife later grew very happy about the business, as his income soared to triple what he had *ever* earned before.

Make sure that you can live for some time with income from some other job or other source until the cash flow begins to come your way in your new business. Ask your upline to be realistic with you about the time frames and income levels you can expect. You do not want to find yourself in a cash-flow bind just when your business begins to blossom. It is wise to replace current income before jumping into network marketing full time because there are ups and downs in the initial stages of the business.

A pound saved is a pound earned
It is important to be able to distinguish among the many spending opportunities that are available to you. Some are true business necessities, some will be appropriate in the future, and some probably never will make good business sense. Tick each of the following spending opportunities and compare your answers with the authors'.

	Buy now	Not now	Maybe never
1. An accounting package to put your business's accounting information on your personal computer.	____	____	____
2. A personal computer for your accounting package.	____	____	____

	Buy now	Not now	Maybe never
3. A large car for moving people to meetings.	___	___	___
4. Key products for your own use and for sale to others.	___	___	___
5. An office outside the home to impress others.	___	___	___
6. Basic training tapes and materials.	___	___	___
7. The complete video package that claims to market the business.	___	___	___
8. Limited quantities of recruiting materials that have been recommended by your upline.	___	___	___
9. Five hundred product/company brochures.	___	___	___
10. Ten product/company brochures.	___	___	___

Answers: 1. Not now 2. Not now 3. Maybe never 4. Buy now 5. Maybe never 6. Buy now 7. Maybe never 8. Buy now 9. Not now (maybe never) 10. Buy now.

Step 5: Build Your Prospect List

Who do you know?

A key tool in the network marketing business is your prospect list. In order to be efficient and effective in getting your message to as many people as possible, you start by putting together a list of names and phone numbers of everyone who should hear about your products, and about this extraordinary business opportunity.

There are some people who you will be hesitant to call. Be sure to put them on your prospect list. We call this our 'chicken list' because we are too chicken to call them, probably because we think that they are too successful to listen to what we have to say. Ironically, they are also the ones most likely to succeed because they have been successful in the past; so be absolutely sure your chickens are on your list!

Before you start calling your prospects, consider ordering three-way calling from BT. (The present cost (1995) is £3.40 per quarter plus VAT. Contact Network Services three-way calling.) With this aid you can talk to a prospect and an experienced upline distributor at the same time. Therefore, chickens on your list can be called with someone who is successful already in the business and who is not scared of your chicken because it is not their chicken.

Prospect list

Product	Friends	Opportunity
1 _____	Family	1 _____
2 _____	Business	2 _____
3 _____		3 _____
4 _____	Acquaintances	4 _____
5 _____	Neighbours	5 _____
6 _____	Referrals	6 _____
7 _____		7 _____
8 _____	Service providers	8 _____
9 _____	People you used to	9 _____
10 _____	know:	10 _____
11 _____	• school	11 _____
12 _____	• former jobs	12 _____
13 _____	• old neighbours	13 _____
14 _____	• former spouse	14 _____
15 _____	• Yellow Pages	15 _____
16 _____		16 _____
17 _____		17 _____
18 _____		18 _____
19 _____		19 _____
20 _____		20 _____
21 _____		21 _____
22 _____		22 _____

Rules

1. Do not edit your success.
2. Retail supports recruiting; recruiting supports retail.

After you have learned the basics of recruiting and role played with your upline, you'll start to make calls. You may wish to get on the phone with your upline and let them make the presentation or invitation to a meeting.

If you want to build a successful business fast, generate a long list of people, the longer the better — 150–300 names if possible — although the names may not occur to you all at once. Many people feel at first that they do not have a large 'circle of influence' or 'do not know anyone'. Many shy, private people have become enormously successful in network marketing, but they had first to get focused about the number of people they have known over the years even in a passing way. In this business those with the biggest prospect lists win. Not because they know so many people, but because they decided to make the world a prospecting environment.

Keep this list simple: names and phone numbers, and keep it with you always. If you are serious about the business, you will start to add names continuously as you meet people at the office, shop, supermarket or dry cleaners.

Whatever you do, avoid keeping names on little pieces of paper or on cards. Your prospect list is your most important practical tool in the day-to-day operation of your business. Every opportunity prospect should be told about the products, and every retail customer should be told about the opportunity.

A key factor in network marketing is that it has little or no capital investment. Thus, people get involved, wanting the utmost income that is possible. However, if they are operating their network marketing business as a hobby, it's little wonder that they do not achieve the incomes they've dreamed about. Even though there is not a capital risk, one needs to treat this as a real and serious business with huge national, perhaps international, potential. So operate it like a business. Keep a prospect list and take action by calling prospects every day to build a group of people interested in the products and the business.

Prospect list (Insert to Daily Planner)

Date Contacted	Name	Phone Number	Comments

This does not mean that you need to do this full time at all. It simply means that when you do it, you need to do it full tilt. This kind of business can be done successfully part time but not spare time.

Become a Network Marketing Leader

The single best way to become a leader in network marketing is to do the business energetically until you find what works, and then have an unbending commitment to pass on what you've learned.

To teach, train and coach your downline organisation, focus on three basic concepts:

1. This is a business of duplication
2. Teach the basics
3. Be available

This is a business of duplication

The power of this business is gearing, in which you get a percentage of other distributors' efforts and corresponding geometric growth in the organisation by enabling people to do a simple process and teach it to others. People will learn that process primarily *by watching you*. In reality, they will not listen much to what you say, they will learn from what you *do* and *don't do*. Therefore, you need to be doing the business exactly the way you want others to do it, or else you will have a trail of ineffectual activity down numerous lines of people. So, the first rule in managing your downline is, *do what you would have others do* — lead by example.

In fact, managing a downline is a misconception. Once the downline is initially developed, we begin to spend time talking with distributors, advising them, analysing them, mistakenly believing that we will not have to get back on the phone and continue to build our organisation through recruiting and retailing. This is a major mistake that almost everyone makes. Instead, *show them* what they should be doing, by staying glued to the phone yourself, and by always bringing new people into the business. When you have new people at the meeting each week, your downline *sees* you doing this and then learns to do it themselves.

What is the best example in life that you have seen of duplication? _____

_____

Is this a good analogy to the network marketing business?

_____

Why?_____

Teach the basics

What each new distributor and what each senior distributor actually needs is *the basics*. Teach and remind them of setting goals, making enough calls daily, building rapport, handling objections and closing sales. Remember, repetition is a good teacher.

Signs and symptoms

Test your awareness of your and your downlines' progress. Tick the box by the appropriate statement. If there are any ticks in the 'symptoms' column, be sure to schedule time to discuss your assessment.

Early signs of success	Early symptoms of a drop-out
☐ Asks lots of questions	☐ Asks few or no questions
☐ Writes down goals	☐ Does not write down goals
☐ Starts thinking of prospect list immediately	☐ Does not make an adequate prospect list
☐ Loves it when upline calls	☐ Says 'What can I do for you?' when upline calls
☐ Calls prospects and upline daily	☐ Makes few if any calls
☐ Is very coachable, really listens	☐ Says or thinks 'I'll do it my way.'
☐ Has a dream	☐ Has no burning desire

On the following page is a checklist of items that are basic to the business and are critical to your downline.

The 15 basics checklist for coaching downline

For instructions on using this checklist, refer to pages 71 and 72.

	1	2	3	4	5	Comments
	C S	C S	C S	C S	C S	
1 Goals						
2 Use of Product						
3 Prospect List						
Daily Calls						
4 Knowledge						
5 Inventory						
6 Training						
7 Tapes						
8 Personal Volume						
Retail Customers						
9 Recruiting/						
Role Playing						
10 Objections &						
Closing						
Role Playing						
11 Three-Way Calling						
12 Honouring Update						
13 Staying Connected						
14 Increasing Self-Esteem						
15 Maintain a Positive Attitude						

Using the 15 basics

The 15 basics checklist is an important tool to use to keep yourself and your downline on track. Use the checklist for yourself as you review each numbered item. When you have a downline, use this checklist with them as well. As you review each item with your downline, tick the boxes under the C (coach) column and S (student) column.

This is a very effective tool – use it often.

---

1. **Goals.** Are your goals tangible and exciting? (Without goals, why go through the tough times?)

2. **Use of product.** Do you use all the products and love them? (Without belief in the products, they will not get far.)

3. **Prospect list/Number of daily calls.** Do you have a *long* prospect list? Are you making numerous calls per day? (Nothing replaces massive action.)

4. **Knowledge about products and company.** Are you learning all about the products and the company? (Knowledge breeds confidence.)

5. **Stock.** Do you have stock appropriate to your goals? (Do you have a stock level that could be sold in one month?)

6. **Training.** Do you go to meetings and training sessions regularly and avail yourself of every training tool possible? (The more training, the more chance of success.)

7. **Tapes.** Do you know about the latest tapes? (Much of our learning and recruiting occurs through audio tape, because tapes are efficient.)

8. **Personal volume/Retail customers.** Do you have an appropriate level of personal sales volume coming in part from retail customers? (This is the backbone of your business.)

9. **Recruiting.** Do you know how to recruit? (Role playing with your upline helps to build skills.)

10. **Handling objections and closing.** Do you know how to handle objections? Are you afraid to close? (Again, role playing is a powerful teaching tool.)

11. **Three-way calling with upline.** Do you have three-way calling on your phone? (Three-way calling allows you to learn how to make calls *live* in real time, first with your upline, and later you teach your downline while you are on the call with their prospects and they can listen in.)

12. **Honouring upline.** Do you honour your upline? (You do not need to love or even like your upline, but it is important to treat them with respect and keep communication open.)

13. **Staying connected with the organisation.** Are you connected to your upline, to your downline, and to the company? Do you go to meetings and gatherings regularly? (Do not underestimate the power of staying connected.)

14. **Increasing self-esteem.** Are you working on increasing your self-esteem? (We can all always increase our self-esteem. This is important in part because this is a business of attracting other people and others are attracted to those who like themselves.)

15. **Maintaining a positive attitude.** Do you monitor your basic attitude? (Once the business information is understood, the biggest challenge is to keep a positive attitude.)

Be available

The final area that you should keep your eye on in working with your downline is that you 'be available'.

What that means is that you have a way to get messages when you are not present, and that you answer those messages quickly. It means that you do three-way calls with your downline. It means that you are present at all meetings. It means that you give your downline the feeling and the knowledge that they are important to you and that their issues and concerns matter.

PART 4
THE DAY-TO-DAY
BUSINESS

Retailing Products and Gaining Customers

Everyone in a legitimate network marketing organisation does some retailing. How much you retail depends on your goals. For instance, if you are using this to make a car payment or pay some bills, then your time can be spent mostly or completely on retailing.

If, on the other hand, you want the income from this business to replace your current income or you want financial freedom, then retailing will become a smaller segment of your time, just as heads of international businesses do not often do all the direct sales of their company's products. The larger incomes in network marketing come from *gearing*, from doing some retailing and then by recruiting and teaching many other people how to use the products and sell them.

Building a retail customer base

Retailing is a simple process. The following steps will bring you your retail business:

1. **Build your prospect list.** Continuously build a prospect list with people who you think will enjoy your products and your business.

2. **Make calls.** Phone someone and, with *enthusiasm*, tell them briefly about your business and/or products.

3. **Invite someone to a product presentation.** Suggest getting together to show the products at no obligation. Schedule a meeting or visit on neutral ground or on your territory (never at their house or office).

4. **Make the presentation.** At the meeting, highlight the *benefits* of your products. People need to learn why they will be better off with your products.

5. **Close.** Ask for their business. Assume that the person wants to experience these great products. If you have done your job well enough in teaching them about the *benefits* of the product, they should be practically asking how to get started on the products.

6. **Mention the business opportunity.** At some point, mention that there is a business opportunity available. Those distributors who forget to do this may one day find that their retail customer is in someone else's organisation.

Maintaining satisfied customers

Once you have made a sale, serve that customer, and that volume, month after month. Tell your customers that you will call on a regular basis. Then use a reminder file and call, periodically, to see if they are happy, if they have any concerns, what they are ready to reorder, etc. Suggest additional products for them to try. Remember, service is the key to success in retailing.

If your company has an automatic reorder option, get your customers on to it. The customer is often happier on an automatic reorder system, feels better taken care of by the company, and you are relieved of involvement in day-to-day handling.

Retailing is important

You get to know your customers
It keeps your finger on the pulse of the market, what the

customer likes, wants, needs and what changes or preferences are occurring in the market.

It duplicates volume
Large volumes come from many people doing a little. Teach your entire organisation how to do some retailing simply and efficiently while building the organisation, thereby reproducing small volumes in large quantities.

Remember, the people who decide to do network marketing in a major way, in time, become like master franchisors ... they spend most of their time teaching others how to run a successful, duplicable small business.

Recruiting to build an organisation

Some people have concerns about recruiting such as being afraid to approach people or not wanting to be a salesperson with their friends and neighbours. In reality, we are all recruiters. We are recruiting to our business, to ourselves, to an idea or to a way of life almost all the time. Recruiting is simply inviting someone else to look at something that you have, that you love, and that you believe in.

The same is true for any business – in order to grow, you need to be in a recruiting mode to attract and teach the best talent so that your organisation can thrive under your leadership and theirs.

Let's look at how to recruit key players. In network marketing we can *not* determine who the winners or big players will be by knowing their education, business background, age, sex, race or nationality. None of these is a determining factor for success in this business. Instead, the determining factors are:

WINNING FACTORS

1. Positive personality
2. Willingness to learn
3. Burning desire
4. Consistent persisting action.

Prospecting and inviting

Most recruiting is accomplished on the phone because that is a very efficient way to sift for interested people. You can invite your friends, acquaintances, or prospects to any of the following:

- Your house
- A luncheon meeting
- Someone else's house
- A hotel meeting
- A conference call
- To listen to a tape

The purpose of your call is to allow the person to see enough possibility of something good for themselves that they decide to come along and investigate. That is all you need to accomplish. Do not try to give someone the entire business over the phone. This is nearly impossible, and is the wrong objective for the call.

You may also invite someone to look at your business when you are at the gym or the supermarket, or after a business meeting. Again, the only purpose of your conversation is to get them to agree to be in front of the entire presentation, so that they can really understand what it is you have to offer. Do not enlarge on the opportunity, just invite – with enthusiasm! Let their curiosity do its job of getting them to the presentation. Too much said in advance satisfies the curious nature and stops people from coming.

The words we use represent less *than 10 per cent* of our effectiveness in recruiting. So, what's the other 90 per cent? See below:

Seven-point recruiting strategy

1. Build rapport
2. Show enthusiasm
3. Carry a positive posture and stance
4. Hold a vision of success

5. Create interest and curiosity
6. Focus on contributing
7. Keep up your volume.

1: Build rapport
Always chat up first (in both warm and cold markets). In other words, build a rapport, a relationship of trust.

Your prospects must feel good about you and have a rapport with you before they can begin to hear what you have to say. You may find that the timing is not right for someone.

There are three basic ways to make rapport:

Compliment (not flatter) **your prospect**. The compliment must be sincere.

Examples:

- 'You'd be perfect for this business.'
- 'You were always a pleasure to work with.'
- 'Nobody has more integrity than you.'
- 'I want your opinion because I think so highly of you.'

Make sure that you feel real about the compliment.

Find something in common. The acronym FORM (**F**amily, **O**ccupation, **R**ecreation and **M**oney) is a helpful way to remember how to find common ground.

Examples:

- 'Are you a skier?' 'A runner?' 'A weight lifter?' 'A reader?' 'A walker?' 'A tennis player?' 'A golfer?'
- 'What do you do?'
- 'Do you love what you do?'
- 'Does that make you as much money as you want?'

Remember, you want your contact to be real and to make sense. You will become more proficient at chatting people up over time.

Show interest and excitement in the other person. When you are interested in them, you are interesting to them.

Examples:

- 'That's terrific ...'
- 'How interesting; tell me more ...'
- 'What's important to you in life?' 'What's missing?'

2: Show enthusiasm
Enthusiasm excites. Enthusiasm generates interest and creates curiosity. Enthusiasm sells!

Remember: A sale is a transfer of enthusiasm
Examples:

- 'I'm involved in a new and exciting business ...'
- 'I've found something that you have to see ...'
- 'I've got something that I can't wait to show you ...'

If you are dull, you are not attractive, and that is not what you are trying to communicate.

3: Carry a positive posture and stance
Posture and stance are a major key to success. You need to hold several background beliefs to have the right strength and stance. Some of these are belief in the:

√ Extraordinary nature of the business opportunity
√ Superiority of your products
√ Value and importance of your business
√ Direction you are going and that the other person should come along
√ Urgency of developing your business now
√ Business and that it is appropriate for the prospect
√ Ability you have to bring this person to success in your business.

Examples:

- 'This is too important to wait ...'
- 'You're busy? Cancel it ...'
- 'No, I'm not going to send you some literature; what I will do is send you an audio tape − but I'm posting it first class only if you promise me you will listen to it in the day you get it and we'll talk the next day. Is that a promise? You have to hear about this ...'
- 'This is by invitation, I'm reserving you a seat. So tell me now if you're not going to be there. If there is a possibility that you'll cancel, let's not make the appointment. I'll be there for you. I'm putting it in my diary ...'
- 'That's what I thought at first, too. Think about it this way ...'

4: Hold a vision of success
You need to hold a vision of success in your mind for your prospects.

Visualise the person you are talking to:

- Signing the distributor agreement
- As a success in your business
- Happily involved in spending their money on what they want and being free to go where they want during the day.

5: Create interest and curiosity
People come to a meeting out of curiosity. People don't come when they think they know what it is. Do not say too much when you invite − do not satisfy the curiosity. This is not done out of deception; it is rather with the intent of letting the person see the entire presentation intact, which is nearly impossible to do over the phone.

Examples:

- 'Wait till you see this. This situation is extraordinary.'
- 'It's too important to talk about over the phone.'

- 'There is a fascinating presentation that takes about an hour. It's on the cutting edge.'

6: Focus on contributing

Each time you interact with someone, remember to keep your eye on that person's well-being. The question becomes, 'What's good for that person?', not 'Is the person going to make me money?' When you are focused on contributing to other people, the business and the income are natural outcomes.

Keeping an attitude of contribution is not easy. It is one of the ironies of this business.

Think of the business as a gift for your prospect. Do not think of your prospect as money for yourself. If you can think of your prospect's happiness and best interest, your own money will come.

7: Keep up your volume of contacts

Volume of contacts is critical to success. If you dream and hope but do not take regular and consistent *action*, nothing is realised in this business.

You need to talk to several people each day to generate enough activity to grow a real business instead of a hobby.

You are sifting the population to find those few people who are entrepreneurial and willing to work for their dreams. If you want to create a large business, we recommend you make at least 12 contacts per day, so that you develop and keep activity in progress always. The more people you talk to, the bigger your business will grow. Other kinds of recruiting businesses, like personnel recruitment, insurance and stock brokerages require significantly higher contact-per-day numbers, and they have less residual income potential.

PART 5
PROSPECTING

How to Prospect

The more you like someone, the higher they should be in the order of who you should talk to first. You want to make sure that you have a *written* prospect list of no fewer than 150 to 300 people. This list will consist of two main types of people, warm and cold.

Your prospect lists

Warm list
1. Family and friends
2. Business and personal acquaintances
3. Other people with whom you have connections
4. Referrals
5. List of names where you have a rapport – school, clubs, organisations, etc
6. Friends' lists – corporate, organisational.

Cold list
1. 'Walk and talk' around town, meeting new friends
2. Meeting strangers – while doing daily activities
3. Using other people's circle of influence.

Remember: The purpose of the contact is to invite the person to a meeting.

√ Do not underestimate your existing circle of influence (warm list). This is statistically likely to produce the most results for you.

√ Get good at asking for referrals, so that you never run out of warm market prospects.

√ Work in the warm market until you have called everyone in your warm list. Do not jump to walking and talking too fast, because the statistics show that you need to make more contacts in your cold market than in your warm market. You will eventually get good at both markets.

Types of prospect for initial contact

There are numerous types of prospect, each of which might merit a slightly fine-tuned approach, such as:

- Close relative
- Not-so-close relative
- Active, close friend (in touch recently, know each other well)
- Inactive, close friend (friend, but haven't been in touch for a while)
- Inactive, former friend (used to have a close relationship, but haven't been in touch in a long time)
- Active acquaintance/personal (seen recently or often, but do not know well)
- Active acquaintance/business
- Cold call: related in some way (school, club, etc)
- Cold call: unrelated (phone book, etc)
- Stranger
- Long distance (various types of relationship).

The referral approach

You can also take an indirect approach in your conversations, asking people who they know who might be interested in a business; they will probably refer someone to you and/or they speak up about themselves.

The basic conversation
We recommend that you tend to lead with a conversation

about the business instead of the products during times of high growth, and when you are first building the infrastructure of your organisation, because it tends to be more efficient in sifting for entrepreneurs. Leading with the products is also a legitimate alternative.

Sample conversation:

- 'How are you?' 'How are the kids?'
- 'How's business?'
- 'How's the job?'
- 'Would you be interested in a new business opportunity or possibility?'
- 'Would you be interested in a second source of income for your family?'
- 'Would you be interested in earning some extra money?'
- 'Would you be interested in the potential for financial freedom? I'm involved with a business that you have to see.'

Work on making the referral conversation your own.

The referral conversation
'I'm with a company that is in a high growth mode now. I'm an executive,' and 'I'm doing some recruiting today. The top people in my business make more money than most people can think of.' 'I'm looking for a few key people to work with in this geographic area. I'm looking for two or three people who might come to your mind who might appreciate a call like this, who might be unhappy where they are, not making enough money, or are just looking for an extraordinary business alternative. I will treat them courteously, and if they are interested I will invite them to a formal business preview as a guest — if they are not interested I will take up no more of their time.'

When you get a name the following is a good example of what to say:

'Shelley, Kim Lee gave me your name and said that you were

---

quite entrepreneurial and a go-getter (or whatever was said about the person). She thought that you would be interested in hearing about a business opportunity. I'm with a company that went from £_____ to £_____ turnover.

If they say they are interested themselves, you can follow with:

'You say you might be interested – tell me a little bit about yourself,' or 'I've got slots on Tuesday at 2 pm or Wednesday at 4 pm, or, better still, why don't you come to our business preview on _____ at _____ Hotel? Just come to the registration desk and say you are my guest, otherwise they will charge you. If you say you are coming, I will be waiting for you.'

Create your own beginning dialogue

Who are you pretending to talk to?_____

Relationship to you?

☐ relation   ☐ friend   ☐ acquaintance   ☐ cold

How will you begin? _____

_____

_____

_____

What are you asking them for (or asking them to do)? _____

_____

_____

_____

Ask for an appointment. _____

_____

Doing the presentation

In making your formal business presentation, do what has *proved to be successful* for others. Locate the successful people in your upline organisation and learn everything you can from them. Watch how they do the presentation, and with their permission, use that same presentation. If they have developed materials for you, use those. Later on, once you really know the business, put your own personality, style and emphasis in and change accordingly. But, initially, stick with tried and true methods and experience.

If you are too shy to do a presentation yourself do not worry. Ask your upline to do it for you, or to help you. You can also often plug into existing presentations in hotels or phone calls. Or you can use a video or audio tape if necessary. Learn how to present as soon as possible because network marketing is a leadership business.

Points to remember

The following points are important to remember about a presentation:

- **Be enthusiastic.** Your enthusiasm is contagious – the more you have, the more they get.

- **Keep to a one-hour limit.** Do not spend more than one hour on the presentation; people cannot listen much longer.

If you have done a good job, people will stay around to get more information after the formal presentation. Plan your presentation well; remember concise is effective.

- **Speak to prospect's hot button.** Tailor the conversation towards what is important to your prospects and what might be missing in their lives.

- **Close.** Be sure to actually, specifically invite the person to become a distributor. Most sales are lost because the prospect is never asked if they are interested in buying.

Don't let objections dampen your enthusiasm.

Understanding and overcoming objections

Whenever you introduce someone to a new concept or a new product, and particularly, to a new business, that person will have objections. Objections are normal. Do not be surprised or scared by them.

What are objections really? Objections are generally one of five things:

- A *request* for more information. For example, 'Is this a pyramid?'
- A legitimate *concern*. For example, 'I'm not a salesperson.'
- A *smoke screen* hiding the real, hidden concern. For example, 'I'm too busy.'
- A *polite put-off* because they have not seen the value for themselves of what you are saying. For example, 'I'll think about it.'
- A *test* of your belief and knowledge level. For example, 'You can't really make any money doing this.'

Once you understand objections, and understand that they are part of a legitimate investigative process, you can learn how to overcome them. There is a saying that the average sale is made after the fifth objection, and the average salesperson gives up after the second objection.

What you need to do is educate your prospect, taking care of their concerns, matching their goals in life with what you are offering. Persist, until the person gets what they need to make an informed decision.

The following are a few examples of ways to respond to an objection. There are countless other ways that are not given here and that will occur to you as you gain experience.

Objection: *'It's too expensive.'* (Remember, expect a price objection whenever marketing anything, because it is always more expensive than if they bought nothing.)

Response: (The key here is to make sure that the person perceives more value in what is offered than in the money it costs, so talk about the *benefits* to the individual.) *'Haven't you usually found that when it comes to quality you get what you pay for?'*

Objection: *'I'm too busy,'* or *'I don't have any time.'*

Response: *'I know how you feel, I felt exactly the same way.* (Tell your story here.) *That's why I invited you. What I have found is that successful people tend to be busy people. The wonderful thing about the business is that you can get it started and growing on a few hours a week.'*

Objection: *'I have no money.'*

Response: *'That's why I got involved in this business. There is little or no capital risk. Unlike other businesses, it does not take a large investment to get the chance for large financial return.'*

One of the interesting things about objections is that they are quite limited. Your organisation will give you guidance about handling this limited number of objections.

Objections can come fast and look hard, but if you stick them out and stay with an educational approach, giving the facts as you know them, your business should stand up to scrutiny and satisfy the questioning nature of all good prospects.

People have a right, and perhaps a duty to themselves, to ask a lot of questions if they are going to commit their time and energy to something. Remember, objections are limited, just satisfy them, outlive them and you will succeed.

Overcoming your own objections

1. What is your biggest concern or objection before participating in this business?

   _____

   _____

2. What would relieve that concern or handle that objection?

   _____

   _____

3. So what actions will you take?

   _____

   _____

Achieving the sale

To achieve the sale, simply ask for a decision. Nobody likes to make decisions because decisions create the potential for being *wrong* and for failing. Thus, the natural inclination is to 'study' or 'think about it', or just forget about what you're offering them. So if you don't ask for a decision, a person won't make one.

People do not like to be pushy. But do remember that you are not powerful enough to make someone do something that they do not want to do. Your job is to make it easy and less painful to say 'Yes' when they want to go for it.

Asking for the decision will call up hidden objections and will help the prospect to get closer to the true thoughts and feelings about the business. Many people in this business say that they have five to ten people 'thinking about it'. But the reality is that they actually stop thinking about it when they have left the room. So you need clarity and completion, as does your prospect.

Bringing the customer to the point of placing an order may be known as 'closing' the sale. It is a delicate moment experienced in various situations, for example, when we ourselves make decisions to:

- sign a new distributor
- make a purchase
- come to a training session.

Someone may prompt us to agree by saying the right word at the right time or even staying quiet while we think the matter over.

Asking for the decision will call up hidden objections and will help the prospect to get closer to the true thoughts and feelings about the business.

Do not talk past the moment when your person is ready to decide. Many people keep on persuading beyond the 'moment of yes', and then that moment never comes again.

Conclusion

Network marketing is not a complex business. Unlike most businesses, there is very little capital risk. You do not have to analyse it as much as you would if big money was at stake.

With little or no capital risk, the questions become simple: Is this the company I'd be proud to be associated with? Are the products able to capture an appropriate segment of a market? Can I believe in them? Will I enjoy doing the business on a day-to-day basis? All of these are answered simply by trying – experiencing both the products and the business.

A convergence of trends is making network marketing stand out as a business today. The downsizing of corporations, the ageing of the population, the reduction of effectiveness of advertising as an approach to the consumer, the ease and speed of communication technology, the increase of enterprise, and many other trends have positioned network marketing for a staggering boom in the next decade.

Network marketing is fast becoming the single most powerful distribution growth area in business today, both nationally and worldwide. Ultimately, however, the underlying reason for the extraordinary attractiveness of network marketing is lifestyle – the potential for individual, economic, and time freedom.

One of the most appealing aspects about this business is that it provides a level playing field – productivity, not capital or politics, matters. Anyone can get involved, and if network marketing is done well enough and long enough, anyone has a chance to become prosperous.

Network marketing is not an easy road; you have to work hard. But have you ever seen anything real or worthwhile where you did not have to work? You need to choose your corporate vehicle carefully, and then remember that if you want a big business, you cannot treat this like a hobby. The one 'flaw' in the industry is that we do not have a capital investment, and so people often lose track of the need for intense, regular, business-like effort to achieve significant success.

If you choose this industry, you are about to embark on a wonderful adventure in business and in personal development. There is no replacing or even approaching the economic potential that comes from creating a source of geared income. And, ironically, there is no way to help other people grow a people-oriented business without becoming a bigger person yourself.

Good Luck and Happy Network Marketing!

Further Reading from Kogan Page

Be Your Own Boss: A Daily Express Guide, David McMullan
Empathy Selling: The Powerful New Sales Technique for the 1990s,
   Christopher G Golis
How to Sell More: A Daily Express Guide, Heil Johnson
*Multi-Level Marketing: A Practical Guide to Successful Network
   Selling*, 2nd edition, Peter Clothier
Network Marketing: A Daily Express Guide, David Barber

Inexpensive paperbacks covering all areas of personal
development and basic management. Practical, easy to read
and instantly accessible, these guides will help people to
improve their business or communication skills. Those marked
* are available on audio cassette. A selection is listed below.
For further details, please contact the publisher Kogan Page,
telephone 0171 278 0433, fax 0171 837 6348.

Business Etiquette
Effective Meeting Skills
Effective Presentation Skills
Get Organised!
Goals and Goal Setting
How to Communicate
   Effectively*
How to Develop a Positive
   Attitude*

How to Develop Assertiveness
How to Motivate People*
Make Every Minute Count*
Memory Skills in Business
Speed Reading in Business
Successful Negotiation
Successful Telephone
   Techniques